Contents

My First Words 🎧 Track 1
Place the stickers.

spring

summer

fall

winter

rain

snow

mountain

fun

Listen and Point 🎧
Track 2

Listen and repeat. Point to what you hear.

It's **fun to play** in the rain.

It's winter.

It's Raining

Hello, pretty flowers! It's spring.

It's fun to play outside.

Everything is green. It's summer.

It's fun to play in the rain.

The mountain wears red and yellow. It's fall.

It's fun to play in the leaves.

Everything turns to white. It's winter.

It's fun to play in the snow.

Look and Match

Match the pictures to the words.

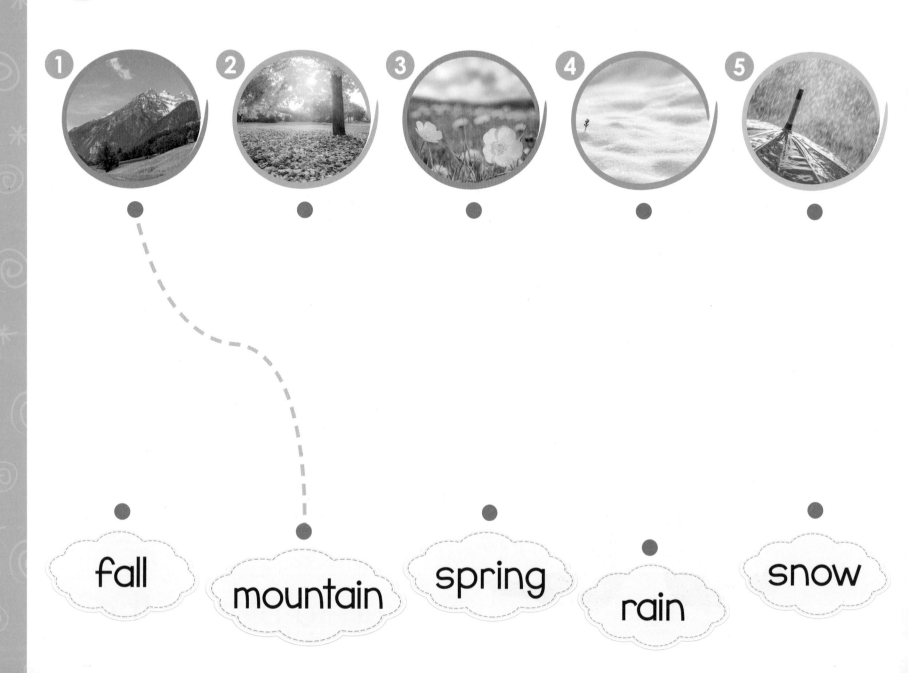

1
2
3
4
5

fall

mountain

spring

rain

snow

Look and Place the stickers
Look at the clues. Then place the word stickers.

Place the stickers

Read and place the correct stickers.

mountain ➔ snow ➔ mountain ➔ rain

rain ➔ snow ➔ mountain ➔ snow

Read and Number

Read the sentences and number. Then say.

1. It's fall!
2. It's spring!
3. It's winter!

Read Aloud

Read the sentences aloud. Repeat and check.

1 It's  .

summer

2 It's .

fall

3 It's fun to play in the .

rain

4 It's fun to play in the .

snow

5 The wears red and yellow.

mountain

Mission

What is your favorite season?
Say your favorite season in English.

☑ **Mission Complete**

Good Job!

My First Words Track 4

Place the stickers.

farm

cow

horse

chicken

zoo

lion

giraffe

elephant

Listen and Point Track 5

Listen and repeat. Point to what you hear.

1

Cows give me milk **every morning.**

2

A lion greets me **with a smile.**

A Farm and A Zoo

Track 6

I like the fresh air at the farm.

Chickens give me eggs every morning.

Cows give me milk every morning.

Horses give us rides every day.

I like the fun mood at the zoo.

A lion roars and greets me with a smile.

A giraffe stretches her neck and greets me with a wink.

An elephant lifts his trunk and greets me with a wave.

Look and Match

Match the pictures to the words.

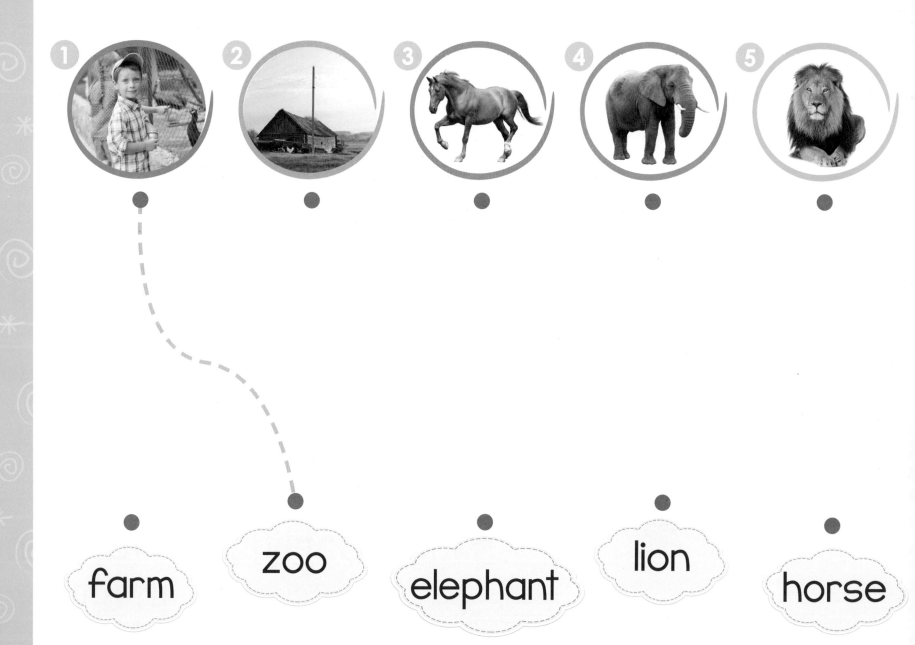

1

2

3

4

5

farm

zoo

elephant

lion

horse

Look and Color

Look and color the farm animals.

1   3 horses

2   1 cow

3   2 chickens

Follow and Place the stickers

Follow the lines and place the zoo animal stickers.

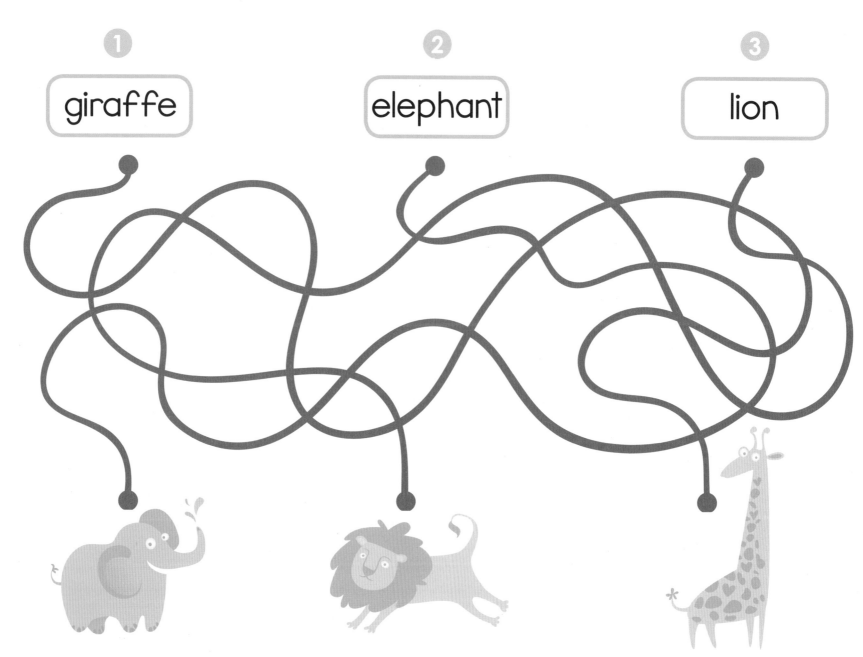

1 giraffe
2 elephant
3 lion

Read and Number

Read the sentences and number the pictures.

1 Chickens give me eggs every morning.

2 Cows give me milk every morning.

3 Horses give us rides every day.

Read Aloud

Read the sentences aloud. Repeat and check.

1.  give me eggs every morning.

   Chickens

2.  give us rides every day.

   Horses

3. A greets me with a smile.

   lion

4. A  greets me with a wink.

   giraffe

5. An greets me with a wave.

   elephant

Mission

Which animals do you like?
Draw one farm and one zoo animal!

☑ **Mission Complete**

Great!

WORDS

My First Words
Track 7

Place the stickers.

sports

ball

track

swimming

basketball

pass

alone

together

Listen and Point Track 8

Listen and repeat. Point to what you hear.

1

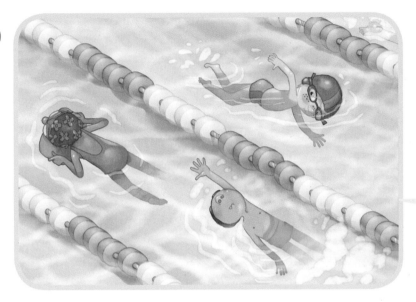

He **is good at** swimming.

2

It's my ball.

It's My Ball

Track 9

Ryan loves to play sports.

He is good at swimming.

He is good at track and field.

He is good at playing alone.

"It's my ball."
Ryan does not pass the ball in basketball.

"It's my ball."
Ryan does not pass the ball in soccer.

So Ryan's coach teaches him how to share.

He becomes good at playing together.
Now, he is happy.

Look and Match
Match the pictures to the words.

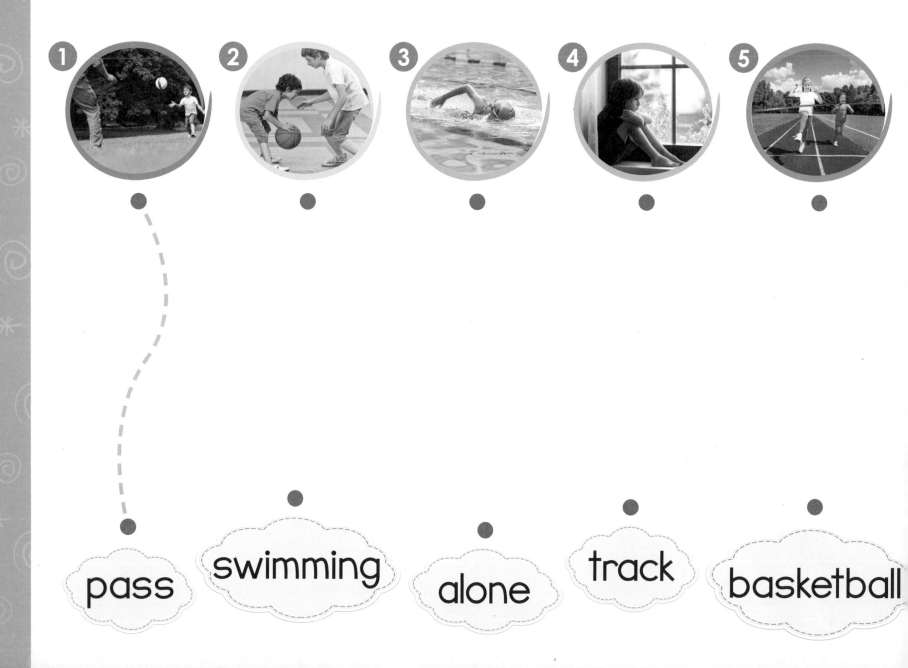

Find and Circle
Find the words for the following pictures.

ball   pass   sports   track   alone

t	r	a	c	k	b
e	p	a	s	s	a
n	p	o	w	t	l
a	l	o	n	e	l
s	p	o	r	t	s

Find and Draw

Find the correct pictures and draw the lines.

basketball

swimming

track

together

Match and Read

Match the correct sentences. Then read.

1

He becomes good at playing together.

2

He is good at track and field.

3

He does not pass the ball in soccer.

Read Aloud

Read the sentences aloud. Repeat and check.

1 It's my .

soccer ball

2 It's my .

basketball

3 He is good at  .

swimming

4 He is good at .

track

5 He is good at playing .

alone

Say three sports you can play together with your friends.

☑ **Mission Complete**

WORDS My First Words Track 10

Place the stickers.

ride

star

trip

moon

rocket

magic

castle

cake

candy

wish

Listen and Point
Track ll

EXPRESSIONS

Listen and repeat. Point to what you hear.

1

I wish I could fly to the moon.

2

Try this moon cake!

A Ride to the Moon

Track 12

Look at the moon and the stars!

I wish I could fly to the moon.

We are in a rocket.

What a magic ride to the moon!

There is a magic castle.

Welcome to the Magic Moon Castle

Try this moon candy!

Try this moon cake!

What an amazing trip to the moon!

Look and Match

Match the pictures to the words.

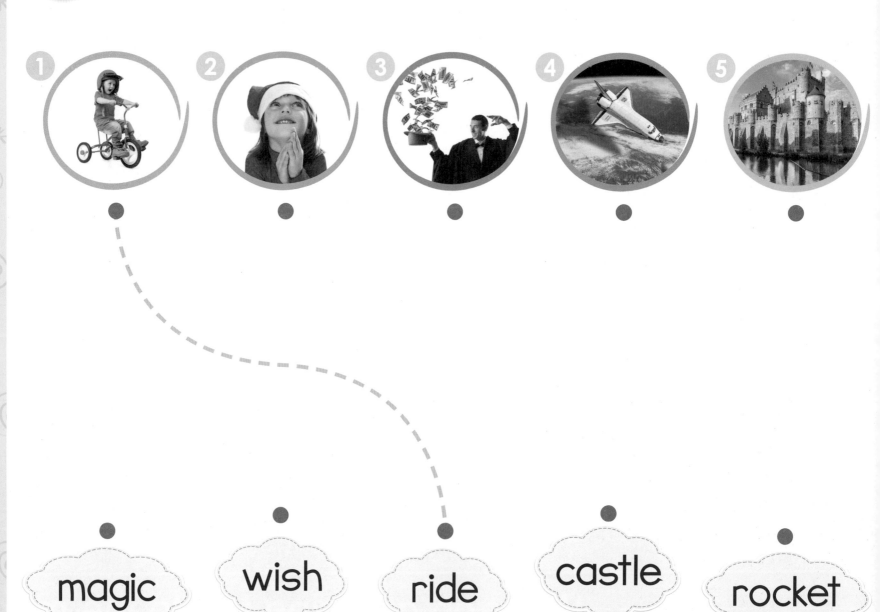

1 2 3 4 5

magic **wish** **ride** **castle** **rocket**

Find and Circle

Find and circle all of the correct pictures.

1 moon

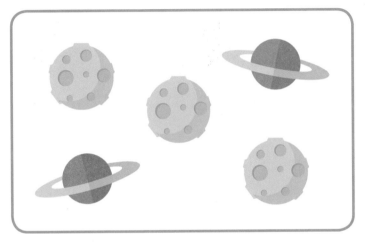

2 star

3 cake

4 rocket

Find and Circle

Find the words for the following pictures.

trip **candy** **ride** **castle** **wish**

s	c	r	i	d	e
c	a	s	t	l	e
b	n	a	r	m	i
u	d	w	i	s	h
o	y	u	p	t	n

Match and Read

Draw lines to finish the sentences and read.

1

I wish I could •

• moon candy!

2

We are •

• moon cake!

3

Try this •

• in a rocket.

4

Try this •

• fly to the moon.

Read Aloud

Read the sentences aloud. Repeat and check.

1 I wish I could fly to the  .

moon

2 I wish I could see the .

stars

3 Try this moon !

candy

4 Try this moon !

cake

5 What an amazing  to the moon!

trip

Mission

Make a wish when you see
a full moon or a shooting star!

☑ **Mission Complete**

Great!

Sing Along

It's Raining

Track 13

Spring! Spring! Spring! It's fun to play out - side.

Summer! Summer! Summer! It's fun to play in the rain.

Fall! Fall! Fall! It's fun to play in the leaves.

Winter! Winter! Winter! It's fun to play in the snow.

A Farm and A Zoo

Track 14

Farm! Farm! Farm! Chickens give me eggs. Cows give me milk.

Zoo! Zoo! Zoo! Roar with the lion. Stretch with the giraffe.

It's My Ball  Track 15

It's my ball! Ball! Ball! Ball! I don't want to pass the ball.

No! No! No! Share the ball with the others.

A Ride to the Moon Track 16

I wish I could fly to the moon. What a magic ride to the moon! What

an a-mazing trip to the moon! Moon! Moon! Moon!

Answer Key

Unit 1 p. 12

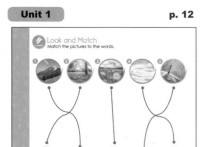

Look and Match
Match the pictures to the words.

fall mountain spring rain snow

p. 13

Look and Place the stickers
Look at the clues. Then place the word stickers.

① winter ② summer
③ spring ④ fall

p. 14

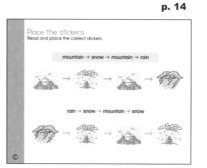

Place the stickers
Read and place the correct stickers.

mountain → snow → mountain → rain

rain → snow → mountain → snow

p. 15

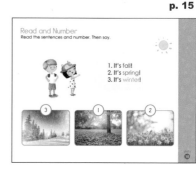

Read and Number
Read the sentences and number. Then say.

1. It's fall!
2. It's spring!
3. It's winter!

3 1 2

Unit 2 p. 28

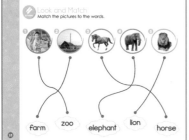

Look and Match
Match the pictures to the words.

farm zoo elephant lion horse

p. 29

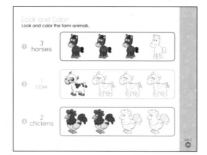

Look and Color
Look and color the farm animals.

① 3 horses
② 1 cow
③ 2 chickens

p. 30

Follow and Place the stickers
Follow the lines and place the zoo animal stickers.

① giraffe ② elephant ③ lion

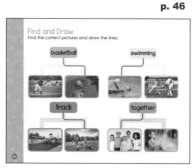

p. 31

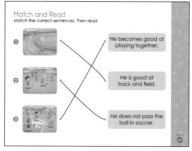

Read and Number
Read the sentences and number the pictures.

1 Chickens give me eggs every morning.

2 Cows give me milk every morning.

3 Horses give us rides every day.

2 1 3

Unit 3 p. 44

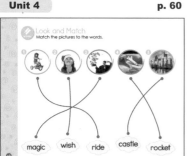

Look and Match
Match the pictures to the words.

pass swimming alone track basketball

p. 45

Find and Circle
Find the words for the following pictures.

ball pass sports track alone

t	r	a	c	k	b
e	p	a	s	s	a
n	p	o	w	t	l
a	l	o	n	e	l
s	p	o	r	t	s

p. 46

Find and Draw
Find the correct pictures and draw the lines.

basketball swimming

track together

p. 47

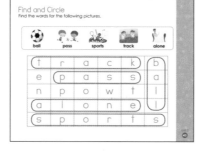

Match and Read
Match the correct sentences. Then read.

① He becomes good at playing together.

② He is good at track and field.

③ He does not pass the ball in soccer.

Unit 4 p. 60

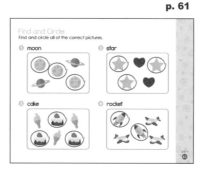

Look and Match
Match the pictures to the words.

magic wish ride castle rocket

p. 61

Find and Circle
Find and circle all of the correct pictures.

① moon ② star
③ cake ④ rocket

p. 62

Find and Circle
Find the words for the following pictures.

trip candy ride castle wish

s	c	r	i	d	e
c	a	s	t	l	e
b	n	a	r	m	i
u	d	w	i	s	h
o	y	u	p	t	n

p. 63

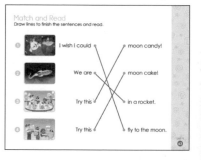

Match and Read
Draw lines to finish the sentences and read.

① I wish I could ———— moon candy!

② We are ———— moon cake!

③ Try this ———— in a rocket.

④ Try this ———— fly to the moon.

p. 2
p. 18
p. 13

winter

fall

spring

summer

p. 14

p. 30

p. 34

p. 50

p. 17

p. 33

p. 49

p. 65

moon

rocket

castle

soccer

basketball

baseball

winter

fall

summer

elephant

lion

horse

spring

seasons

cow

chicken

My First

English 6

trip

star

track

swimming